The Adventures of Phiggy the Piggy:

The Magical Dream

Written By
Deirdre Kennedy and Lee Ann Callaghan

Illustrated By
Bernadette Mercado

Copyright 2017
By Green Bamboo Publishing
Deirdre Kennedy, Lee Ann Callaghan,
And Bernadette Mercado

All rights reserved.

No part of this book may be reproduced in any form without written permission from the publisher.

ISBN 978-0-9959983-1-5

GREEN BAMBOO PUBLISHING
Ontario, Canada

www.greenbamboopublishing.com

Dedicated to J

...

Phiggy was created to inspire an understanding of diversity, take a glimpse into the magical worlds of dreams and emotions, promote animal welfare, and promote the interconnectedness of the heart.

...

A portion of the proceeds from this book will be donated to: The St. Vincent de Paul Society of San Francisco.

Their mission is to offer hope and service on a direct person-to-person basis, working to break the cycles of homelessness and domestic violence.

One magical night, the moon was full and the stars were twinkling and smiling on Phiggy as she walked through the woods.

This little piggy had a long day and was ready to take a really, cozy sleep.

She noticed that everything was suddenly very colorful and bright, but slightly different than before she went to sleep.

"How will I wake up and go back to the real world?" asked Phiggy.

"You must find your magic," said the delightful Faerie,

and pointed her magic wand at Phiggy's heart.

Suddenly many characters started to appear.

Friendly forest folk tumbled through grounds.

Other forest folk were juggling magical balls, while others were making beautiful patterns with amazing toys that Phiggy had never seen before.

A Blue Jay flies by and crashes into a tree!

"Oh, yes, I'm okay. I'm just trying to find my magic," says Blue Jay.

"ME, TOO!" says Phiggy excitedly. "Let's find our magic together."

Shaking hands, Phiggy and Blue Jay walk on through the wonderful dream forest.

Nearby, a naughty Meercat called Joe-Hawk, whose hair was in a big purple mo-hawk, was listening.

He was hiding behind a stone. Alone, and rubbing his hands together, he said,

"I want to find what this magic is all about and steal it from them!"

"My name is Reina,
and I'm here to help you.
What do you need?"

"Oh, we need to find our magic,"
say Phiggy and Blue Jay
at the same time.

"And we don't know
where it is."

"Great!" says Blue Jay.
And together they begin
to create magic.

"I believe in my heart that I have
lots of friends," says Phiggy.

Suddenly, lots of little forest
friends appear. Some of them are
tumbling on the ground. Other friends
have musical instruments and play a
little song for Phiggy.

"I believe in my heart that I am an amazing painter," says Blue Jay.

Suddenly, forest friends appear again and give him a paintbrush, a tin of paint, a little hat, and a canvas.

"We can all create a beautiful dream together!" exclaims Reina.

Then the delightful Faerie looks around and spots something suspicious. Flying over to the big stone, she discovers Joe-Hawk!

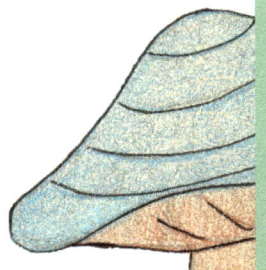

"Gather around my friends," says the delightful Faerie, and she talks at great length about how magic for everything is inside your heart.

Phiggy then knew that if she wanted to wake up, she could ask in her heart at any time.

"I want to wake up and tell all my wonderful friends about this amazing dream," she says.

About Deirdre Kennedy

Deirdre Kennedy is from Ireland and lives in San Francisco since 2000. An avid writer and creative entrepreneur, she also leads sacred tours in Egypt, owns an Art Gallery in San Francisco with family, and is an arts educational charity founder. "I love to help people explore the diverse sacred environment, celebrate their creativity, and inspire children. I'm a goof-ball at heart who loves to make up characters and funny voices, and the Phiggy character was born out of lots of laughs with Lee Ann Callaghan and our shared love for animals and spirituality, and Bernadette beautifully brought our vision to life — dream team! Children are the future of the planet, so I believe that sharing information with them that will help them to be more accepting, loving and excited to nurture their own unique gifts, is of utmost importance." Learn more: www.deekennedy.com

About Lee Ann Callaghan

Born and raised in New Jersey with many life long friends and loved ones, Lee Ann has a strong heart and soul. But more adventures were to be had so at age 30 she got on an airplane and moved with her best friend to the far away unknown land of San Francisco California. As soon as she got off of the plane her soul felt at home. Lee Ann has built a long successful career in Management and truly believes that dreams do come true.

About Bernadette Mercado

Bernadette is a self-taught artist that grew up in the heart of the Mission district in San Francisco. Growing up in the Mission gave her a great appreciation for art at a very early age. As Bernadette grows as an artist, her interest in realism portraits has increased and has become her main art style. Her goal as an artist is to use her art to help others, whether it's to encourage a child to read or to bring a community together by creating a mural.

www.ingramcontent.com/pod-product-compliance
Lightning Source LLC
Chambersburg PA
CBHW042228010526
44113CB00045B/2871